WOLFGANG AMADEUS MOZART

The Greatest Pure Musician the World Has Ever Known

THE HISTORY HOUR

HISTORY

CONTENTS

INTRODUCTION

৩১৪৩

Johannes Chrysostomus Wolfgangus Theophilus Mozart was born in the Archbishopric of Salzburg, a prince-bishopric of the Holy Roman Empire and independent state that would later become part of Austria. His father, Leopold Mozart (1719-1787), was a composer and teacher of great distinction, and his wife, Anne Maria Perti, was the daughter of a distinguished jurist who fell into poverty and died, leaving her, her mother, and her elder sister in dire poverty. When she married Leopold in 1747 though, they were regarded as the most handsome couple in Salzburg, and she was the perfect mother to the young prodigies Nannerl (Mozart's older sister) and Wolfgang. They had seven children, but only two of them survived: Wolfgang and Nannerl, his older sister, who was also a child prodigy and brilliant composer, whose career was cut short because of the focus on Wolfgang.

꧁꧂

Probably the most naturally gifted musician the world has ever known, Mozart began his career early as a child prodigy. By the age five, he was already proficient on the violin and the keyboard (mainly the harpsichord, but also the piano), and had begun composing music that had integrity. He was a showman as well, according to contemporary documents, and charmed many of the crowned heads of Europe with his performance and his manner.

꧁꧂

Unlike other child prodigies though, Mozart developed gradually into a mature musician, composing operas (judged to be the best of the Classical era), concertos (also judged to be among the best of the era), forty-one symphonies (of varying quality; the early symphonies are somewhat unremarkable, but the last twelve are astonishing feats of brilliance), string quartets, piano sonatas, and many other kinds of music. Although he died when he was only thirty-five years old, he is still one of the most prolific composers who ever lived. His late work is far ahead of its time; he focused much of his attention on the music of Johann Sebastian Bach, to whom he had been introduced by the so-called London Bach, Johann Christian Bach, who was one of Bach's sons who made a fortune in London England, and who taught him.

꧁꧂

Mozart's legacy is monumental; he used his gifts brilliantly despite the many setbacks he had in his life, many of which were due to his abrasive character. When he died, he was too poor to afford a proper burial, and he was buried in a pauper's grave, but his wife Costanza Mozart, (nee Weber), made it her life's work to promote Mozart, and his son also kept his memory alive, touring as Mozart.

❧ II ❧
EARLY YEARS OF
PRODIGY

"I pay no attention whatever to anybody's praise or blame. I simply follow my own feelings."

— WOLFGANG AMADEUS MOZART

Mozart was born in the middle of winter, on January 27th, 1756, at eight o'clock in the evening. He was christened a few days later, and within a few years, he began to experiment on the harpsichord, finding successions of thirds. When he was four, his father began to teach him the rudiments of music, and he excelled at an incredible rate, trying out composition. His sister, Nannerl remembers

> "He often spent much time at the clavier, picking out thirds, which he was ever striking, and his pleasure showed that it sounded good.... In the fourth year of his age his father, for a game as it were, began to teach him a few minuets and pieces at the clavier.... He could play it faultlessly and with the greatest delicacy, keeping exactly in time.... At the age of five, he was already composing little pieces, which he played to his father who wrote them down."

According to his father, Leopold, a distinguished teacher, his early compositions, although aided by his father, were his own work. He began writing music when he was five years old, and when he was six years old, he and his family took an extended tour of Europe where he and his sister Maria Anna (known as Nannerl), performed for many of the crowned heads of Europe. He never had any formal education and never attended a school. His father chose to educate him at home in music, Latin, and modern languages (he was fluent in German, Italian, French, and English for all his life.)

THE FIRST TOURS

᠄᠄᠄

When Wolfgang was six years old, in 1762, his family took him on three short concert tours. First, in January, they traveled to Munich, a city that would play a significant part in his career, and both Nannerl and Wolfgang were invited to play for Prince Elector Maximilian III of Bavaria. Then in October, Leopold took the entire family to Vienna, where young Wolfgang "*Amadé*" Mozart performed on October 13th for Emperor Francis I of Austria, who called him "*ein kleine hexenmeister*" (a little magician).

᠄᠄᠄

On October 13th, 1762, Wolfgang and Nannerl performed for Empress Maria Theresa at Schönbrunn Palace. In attendance . were the court composer George Christoph Wagenseil and many of Maria Theresa's sixteen children, including her son Antoine, who was close to the same age as Wolfgang.

According to reports, Wolfgang played the harpsichord very well and was rewarded with one hundred ducats and many gifts from the nobles in attendance. He was also presented with a beautiful outfit that had belonged to Archduke Max, a lilac-colored coat and a moiré waistcoat trimmed with gold braid.

⚜

According to some relatively unreliable sources, when the young prince Antoine sat on his mother's lap, Mozart also climbed on to her lap and declared that he would marry her when he grew up. He also performed some tricks, including playing on a keyboard that had a cloth covering the keys, and he also asked the court composer to give him some music to play. Whether or not this story is true, it is certainly true that young Mozart had become a very popular entertainer because of his performance at the court.

⚜

On December 11th, 1762, the whole family traveled to Pressburg, which is today known as Bratislava, at the invitation of the Hungarian nobility. The roads were so poor, and young Wolfgang was so sick that Leopold bought a new carriage in Pressburg and then on Saturday, December 24th, 1762, the Mozarts left Pressburg at 8:30 in the morning and arrived in Vienna at 8:30 in the evening, on their way home to Salzburg. Mozart showed signs of exhaustion on his short tour, and when they arrived home, Mozart was already ill with rheumatic fever. In fact, Mozart was sick many times in his life, and his father pushed him nonetheless because he saw that his young son was a great attraction to royalty and a great source of income.

❧ III ❧

THE GRAND TOUR 1763-66

"Just as people behave to me, so do I behave to them. When I see that a person despises me and treats me with contempt, I can be as proud as any peacock."

— WOLFGANG AMADEUS MOZART

After these short jaunts, Leopold Mozart decided that it was time to introduce the great child prodigy to the art of touring, and decided on a long, three-year tour of Europe. Over the next three years, Mozart would play in seventeen different cities in seven different countries.

Leopold Mozart wanted to begin the tour as soon as possible, to take maximum advantage of their youth and therefore the wonder of their abilities. Wolfgang was seven at the beginning of this tour and Nannerl was eleven. The planned route included southern Germany, the Austrian Netherlands (i.e., Belgium), Paris, Switzerland and possibly northern Italy, including Rome. The London leg was added after several influential Englishmen pressured him in Paris, and the stop in the Netherlands was totally unplanned. The idea was to take in as many European courts as possible, as well as the great cultural capitals, in the style of the Grand Tour.

Many things had to be planned, given the mercurial nature of royal courts and their paying for these sorts of things. Payment would almost certainly happen, but Leopold could not ask for a specific amount of money, and payment frequently was in the form of some expensive trinket, like a golden snuff box. As useless as these things must have been for a young man, they were payment of a sort and enriched Leopold greatly. Leopold was always a very strong-willed person, and his wife Anna Maria deferred to him despite her strong will. She was not in favor of the tour because Wolfgang had been sick during the short tours they made the year before but supported him.

❧❧❧

Leopold, for his part, relied on his own professional musical network and on the social contacts he had made the year before on the shorter tours to secure invitations from the various royal courts. He had help from his good friend Johann Lorenz Hagenauer, the landlord, business partner, and friend of Leopold. Hagenauer was a major trader, with many connections throughout Europe, and he provided a sort of banking system in which they were able to access money in several cities while waiting for the payment from the various royal families. He also applied to his employer, the Prince, Archbishop, of Salzburg, for an extended leave of absence, which was granted even though he had only just been appointed vice-Kapellmeister in January 1763, because this would bring honor to Salzburg, to the Prince, Archbishop, and to God.

❧❧❧

Young Wolfgang practiced hard on the harpsichord and, according to reminiscences from his father and older sister, he practiced and perfected his technique on the violin without any training from anyone. The two children prepared a number of duets they could play and clearly enjoyed making music together.

❧❧❧

The previous year, Leopold had managed to save the equivalent of two years' salary at his position as vice-Kapellmeister from the trip to Vienna the previous year, and this money was used to finance the grand tour.

FIRST STOP MUNICH

❦

The family set off on June 9th, 1763, in the new carriage they had purchased the year before, and on the very first day, a wheel broke, forcing them to stop for a day in Wasserburg-am-Inn while it was being repaired. Leopold took advantage of this delay by taking Wolfgang to a local church where he introduced the boy to the organ. They reached Munich soon after and proceeded to give four concerts in June, most likely with Mozart and Nannerl playing together in all of them, in the presence of Elector Maximilian III. One of the concerts was on the evening of 13th June 1763, from 8 o'clock until 11 o'clock in the evening. These concerts earned the family nearly two hundred florins.

AUGSBURG

❧

A fter having much success in Munich, the family left on June 22nd, 1763, for Augsburg, where Leopold had many connections because he was born and had grown up there. Leopold's mother, from whom he was estranged, refused to attend any of the concerts. At this time, Wolfgang was still a young boy and grew homesick, waking up several times in the night crying, mentioning specific people from Salzburg whom he missed. The family also gave three public concerts in Augsburg and moved on to the small town of Schwetzingen which was the seat of the famous Mannheim court, which boasted the finest orchestra in Europe. Mannheim was the place where the first orchestras were created, and the symphony was created. Here, the Electors Palatine Karl Theodor and his Electress were very impressed.

FRANKFURT

❦

Following the stop at the Mannheim court, the family went to Frankfurt-am-Main. Leopold wrote about these concerts on August 20th, 1763:

"We played a concert on the 18th which was outstanding. Everyone was thoroughly amazed. Thank God we are healthy and, wherever we go, much admired. As for little Wolfgangerl, he is extremely jolly, but also quite naughty. Little Nannerl is no longer in his shadow, and she now plays with such skill that the world talks of her and marvels at her."

It is a surprising admission, considering the position of women in society at the time that the two children received equal billing.

❦

In Frankfurt, Mozart gave a solo concert, advertised with as much hyperbole as can be expected from a proud father. The advertisement in the Frankfurt newspaper read:

> *"He [Wolfgang] will play a concerto for the violin and will accompany symphonies on the harpsichord. While doing this, the keyboard will be covered with a cloth, and young Mozart will play with as much facility as if he could see the keys; he will instantly name all the notes played at a distance, whether singly or in chords as on the harpsichord or any other instrument, bell, glass, or clock. Finally, he will improvise both on the harpsichord and the organ as long as may be desired and in any key."*

⚜

Also, in Frankfurt, the great writer Johann Wolfgang von Goethe, then fourteen years old, attended a command performance by both children, for which they were paid four Gulden and seven Kreuzers for the opportunity. Johann Peter Eckermann later spoke with Goethe about this meeting. He writes:

> *"I saw him,"*

said Goethe,

> *"at seven years old, when he gave a concert while traveling our way. I myself was about fourteen years old and remembered perfectly the little man, with his frisure and sword. A rare phenomenon like that of Mozart remains a truly inexplicable thing."*

Goethe's memory of Mozart seems accurate. Later on, though, he compared Mendelssohn favorably to Mozart saying that he bore the same resemblance to Mozart as the conversation of a grown man to the "***prattle of a child***."

SMALLER CENTERS

❧

The family then took a trip on a riverboat to Koblenz, Bonn, and Cologne. It is not known if they performed in any of these smaller centers, but they then proceeded westward to Aachen, where they performed for Princess Anna Amalia of Prussia, the sister of Frederick the Great of Prussia. The princess tried to persuade Leopold to abandon his itinerary and go to Berlin to perform for Frederick the Great, but Leopold resisted.

❧

After Aachen, the family traveled to Mainz, where they hoped to perform for the Elector. Sadly, the Elector was ill, and so the family decided to give three public concerts for which they earned two hundred guldens.

❧

Early in September 1763, they reached Koblenz, from where Leopold wrote, almost incredulously, to Hagenauer:

> *"We consort only with aristocrats and other distinguished people. Honestly!"*

BRUSSELS

The family moved on to Brussels on October 4th and stayed for six weeks. Leopold wrote to his friend Hagenauer:

> *"We then stayed in Brussels for three weeks, and Prince Karl [of Lorraine, Governor of the Austrian Netherlands] himself spoke with me and said that he wished to hear my children in a few days, and yet nothing has happened so far. Yes, it looks as if nothing at all will come of it, for the Herr Prince does nothing but hunt, gorge, and booze, and in the end, it turns out that he has no money. In the meantime, I have been unable, from good manners, either to leave here or to give a concert, because on the word of the Prince himself I had to await his decision."*

During this hiatus in Brussels, while waiting for the Prince to stop hunting, Wolfgang began composing. On 14th October, he completed an Allegro for harpsichord, which would later be incorporated into the C major sonata, K. 6, which he finished in Paris.

৩৯৩

Leopold's desire to perform for Prince Karl seems to have been fulfilled, for they gave a concert on November 9th, 1763, that was reported on the *Augspurgische Ordinari-Post-Zeitung* on December 12th, 1763:

> *"What had been reported to us as early as July from the Electoral Court of the Palatinate, and then in August and September from Frankfurt, Mainz, and the Electoral Court in Trier with so many expressions of amazement, we held to be, if not fantastical, then at least exaggerated. Now, however, we have heard with complete astonishment the incomprehensible skill of the two children of Herr Leopold Mozart, vice-Kapellmeister at the Most Serene court in Salzburg, renowned for his own compositions and the publication of the very fine Violin-Schule. Yesterday, the 9th of this month [November], a grand concert took place in the Salle du Concert Bourgeois, attended not only by many nobles, but also by His Royal Highness Duke Carl himself, and all manifested indescribable pleasure."*
>
> *"Now these charming children (who are unique) have traveled to Paris."*

PARIS SUCCESS

꧁꧂

They left for Paris France on November 15th, the capital of classical music at the time, arriving in Paris on November 18th, 1763, and stayed in Paris for five months, housed at the Hotel Beauvais in the rue St Antoine at the home of Count Maximilian Emanuel Franz von Eyck, the Bavarian Ambassador. The Mozarts arrived with a raft of letters of recommendation from nobles, but none of them provided them with the audiences they wanted, except that for Friedrich Melchior Grimm, given to them by the wife of a prominent Frankfurt businessman. Grimm had moved to Paris and become embroiled in many of the artist wars that raged throughout the 1760s and 70s, including the famous Querelle des Bouffons, which established Italian comic opera in Paris. He also decided to take the young family under his wing because of the amazing reviews of their work. As a result of this intercession, the family moved to Versailles on December 24th, and then on 1st January 1764, they finally gave a concert for Louis XV. Indeed, on one particular occasion, when Mozart was dining with the queen, he apparently stood by her, kissing her hand while she fed him pieces of food. The Mozarts' reputation preceded them, and they were feted by the nobility wherever they went.

❧❦❧

At Versailles, they made a point of visiting the famous they also visited the famous mistress to the King, Madame de Pompadour, who was an old woman by this time, although she was, according to Leopold,

> *"an extremely haughty woman who still ruled over everything."*

In Nannerl's later recollections, Wolfgang was forced to stand on a chair and be examined by Madame de Pompadour, and she would not allow him to kiss her.

❧❦❧

Curiously, there is no record of the children giving a formal concert at Versailles. In February 1764, they were given 50 louis d'or (about 550 florins) and a gold snuff-box by the royal entertainments office. This peculiar payment is presumed to be for entertaining the royal family in private, but no further explanation is available. The Mozarts did give private, invitation-only concerts in Paris on March 10th and April 9th at a theatre in Porte St. Honoré.

❧❦❧

Grimm wrote that young Wolfgang as

> *"so extraordinary a phenomenon that one finds it difficult to*
> *believe unless one has seen him with one's own eyes and*
> *heard him with one's own ears."*

Although Mozart began composing the allegro movement to his KV 6 sonata for harpsichord and violin in Brussels while waiting for Karl to summon then, he completed it in Paris, as well as three other sonatas for harpsichord and violin, KV 7, 8, and 9, when he was only seven years old. (KV stands for Köchelverzeichnis, the catalog of Mozart's complete works, compiled by Ludwig von Köchel.)

☙❧

Leopold undertook to have them engraved and published in Paris, including the fact that they were written by a seven-year-old boy, and watched with satisfaction as they sold out their first printing.

☙❧

While in Paris, Nannerl was compared to the greatest virtuosos of the day, but young Wolfgang astonished everyone with his abilities on the piano, violin, and organ. He also not only sight read the arias of Italian and French operas but would transpose them on sight for an audience. He also improvised an accompaniment to a cavatina whose bassline he did not even know. He also began a series of improvisations that were complete works, and he was able to create new pieces on command to the astonishment of the French audiences. He became the darling of Versailles.

☙❧

Mozart met the great Mannheim composer and harpsi-chordist, Johann Schobert, who went around saying mean things about the young virtuoso behind his back, to the chagrin of Leopold who wrote of this tendency to his friend Hagenauer. He also met and befriended the Augsburg born composer Johann Gottfried Eckhardt. It was clear at the time that the music of the Mannheim school, especially Johann Stamitz was very popular, while the other composers, Franz Joseph Haydn, and Johann Christian Bach were being published and widely performed there as well.

❧

After Paris, the family left for Calais on April 10th, 1764, arriving in London on April 23rd, 1764.

LONDON

﴿۞﴾

The first place the Mozarts lived in London was in Cecil Court, near St. Martin-in-the-Fields, above a barbershop. They brought letters of introduction from Paris, which served them very well. In fact, four days after arriving in London, they played for King George III and his young German queen, Charlotte Sophia. Their performance was so successful that they were immediately invited back for May 19th. At this performance, the king asked him to play works by Handel, Johann Christian Bach, and Carl Friedrich Abel. He also accompanied the Queen as she sang an aria, and later, he improvised on the bass line of a Handel aria.

﴿۞﴾

Leopold worked hard to secure concerts for the Mozart children, and, knowing that many of the nobility and gentry of England would leave town for the summer, he also realized that most of them would return for June 4th, the King's birthday, and so he organized a concert for June 5th. After a smashing success at this concert, he sought to get Wolfgang a place at a charity concert for a maternity hospital on June 29th at the Ranelagh Pleasure Gardens. Leopold correctly noted that the English were very fond of charity concerts and figured that this would endear him to the English.

ॐ

Wolfgang was advertised as

> *"the celebrated and astonishing Master Mozart, a child of seven years of age"*

although he was actually eight years old. The notice went on to describe him as

> *"justly esteemed the most extraordinary prodigy, and most amazing genius that has appeared in any age."*

ॐ

Only a week later, Mozart was playing for a private performance at the Grosvenor Square home of the Earl of Thanet. After the concert, Leopold returned home with inflammation of this throat and other acute symptoms. Leopold himself believed he was dying, as he wrote to his friend Hagenauer

> *"prepare your heart to hear one of the saddest events."*

He was, in fact, sick for several weeks, during which time the children did not perform. The family moved to the countryside, to 180 Ebury Street in Pimlico (which was then a separate town, and not in downtown London as it is today!)

☙❧

Wolfgang spent his days composing music at this time since he was unable to perform. At some point during this year in England, Mozart met Johann Christian Bach and was inspired to begin writing symphonies. In any case, he wrote his first symphony during the convalescence of his father. In E flat major, KV. 16, his First Symphony is rudimentary by the standard of his later works, but quite in the style of J. C. Bach. He also began to write his second symphony, (KV 19) in D major, although it was completed in The Hague, later. Although these are the only orchestral works completed during this period, there is much musical evidence to suggest that Mozart was thinking orchestrally quite a lot during this period. Several unfinished sketches survive that suggest that there may have been several other symphonies that he did not complete, written at this time.

☙❧

In addition to these symphonies, Mozart wrote a piano sonata for four hands in C major, KV 19d, a set of violin sonatas with extra flute and 'cello parts, which were dedicated, at her request, to Queen Charlotte, and presented to her in January 1765. Mozart also wrote a motet called "***God is our Refuse***" KV 20 and a tenor aria "***VA, dal furor portata***," KV 21.

☙❧

In September, when Leopold recovered, the family moved

back to London, to 20 Thrift Street (later renamed Frith Street), in Soho. This flat was close to several concert halls and the homes of Johann Christian Bach, the son of Johann Sebastian Bach and music master to the queen, and Carl Friedrich Abel. Bach became a family friend, playing music with Mozart as an equal. Abel may not even have met Mozart, but Mozart certainly knew his symphonies from attending the annual Bach-Abel concert series.

☙❧

On October 25th, King George III invited the two children to play at the celebrations for the fourth anniversary of his accession to the throne. After that, they did not perform in public (they continued to perform for private events) until February 21st, 1765. This was not a stunning success, because it was on the same night as one of the Bach-Abel concerts, a stunning oversight on the part of the elder Mozart. Nevertheless, Leopold reported that

> *"At every court, it's true, we've been received astonishingly graciously but what we've experienced in England outshines the rest."*

☙❧

The Mozarts offered the chance for people to hear Mozart play at his own lodgings; for five shillings, he would perform in private concerts between April and June of 1765. He also performed a public concert on May 13th. During June of 1765, the two "*young Prodigies*" performed every day at the Swan and Harp Tavern in Cornhill, for a fee of two shillings, sixpence. These concerts were planned, and the workload for the young musicians was so heavy to try to recoup the losses incurred by their lack of income during Leopold's convalescence and the exorbitant medical bills. As Leopold reported, young Wolfgang continued to develop as an artist and even he was impressed with the musicianship of his young son. Given this, it was sort of disappointing that the Mozarts were thought of as an oddity, a sort of freak show, in London. And in the true English style, Mozart was examined by the Honorable Daines Barrington, a noted scientist, to measure his unique abilities. Barrington concluded that indeed, Mozart was a singular genius. Before they left for the continent on July 24th, 1765, Leopold donated the score for "***God is our Refuge***" to the British Museum.

THE NETHERLANDS

৩২৬

When the family returned to the continent, they were not healthy. It appears that the weather in England was not beneficial for them as Wolfgang got tonsillitis and Leopold had prolonged dizziness attacks. They were forced to stay for a month in the little town of Lille. Although their specific plan was to return to Paris, these various illnesses forced them to rethink their plan, and Leopold was persuaded by an envoy of the Princess Carolina of Orange-Nassau to go to The Hague as official guests of the court.

৩২৬

Early in September, when all the family had recuperated a little, they moved on to Ghent where Wolfgang played the new organ that had just been installed at Bernardine's chapel, and a few days after that, he played on the cathedral organ in

Antwerp. They arrived in the capital, The Hague, on September 11th, 1765.

⚜

As luck would have it, Nannerl developed a severe cold and could not perform during the first week or for a performance before the Prince of Orange a few days later. However, Leopold was certain enough that Nannerl would recover to put a notice of a concert that would take place on September 30th, 1765, at the hall of the Oude Doelen in The Hague. He placed a notice in the local paper that read:

> *"All the overtures will be from the hands of this young composer [...] Music-lovers may confront him with any music at will, and he will play it at sight."*

⚜

There is no report of the concert ever having taken place, and it is almost certain that Nannerl did not perform as she developed typhoid fever, which was judged to be sufficiently serious that she was given extreme unction on October 21st; the family had come to terms with this loss when the royal physician, Thomas Schwenke intervened and helped her recuperate by the end of October. To their consternation, Wolfgang then fell ill and was not better until mid-December. He had a board placed over his bed so that he could continue composing.

⚜

It appears that the concert advertised for September actually took place on January 22nd, 1766, and it is likely that it was the premiere Mozart's Symphony in D (KV 19) and possibly a new symphony in B-flat major, KV 22, which had been composed as he waited or Nannerl to recover. After this concert, they were very well known in the Netherlands and traveled to Amsterdam for two weeks where they gave two sell-out concerts on January 29th and February 26th, 1766, made up of instrumental music of Wolfgang's own composition, before returning to The Hague in early March.

☙❧

They returned to The Hague to participate in the "*coming of age*" ceremony for the Prince of Orange. Mozart composed a medley of well-known predominantly Dutch songs (called a "*quodlibet*") called "*Gallimathias Musicum*," (KV 32) for a small orchestra and harpsichord accompaniment, which was premiered at a special concert to honor the Prince, on March 11th, 1766. Interestingly, Mozart also wrote several arias for the princess, using the libretto to *Artaserse*, by Metastasio, the most famous Italian librettist of opera seria (this is the term for serious Italian Classical operas), and a series of keyboard variations on a famous Dutch song called "*Laat ons juichen, Matavieren!*" (KV 24), the world's oldest national anthem, and the national anthem of the Republic of The Netherlands. Even at this young age, Mozart was a facile and incredibly quick composer; he rattled off a set of keyboard and violin sonatas dedicated to the Princes, just as he had done for the French princess, and the Queen of England. While he was in Holland, he also wrote another symphony, (KV 45a) which is now referred to as "*Old Lambach*" because it was mistakenly thought to have been written at the Lambach Abbey in Austria in 1679.

☙❧

Leopold was very taken with the financial cash cow that the children had turned out to be, and, rather than go home to his career in Salzburg, took them in March 1766 to some other cities in The Netherlands, including Haarlem, where the organist of St. Bavo's Church invited Mozart to play the largest organ in the country. They continued on their way east and south, giving concerts in Amsterdam and Utrecht in April, and then continuing on through Brussels and Valenciennes, to Paris. They arrived on May 10th.

FINAL LEG OF THE TOUR: PARIS, SWITZERLAND, AND GERMANY

꧁꧂

I n Paris, they again stayed at the residence of the Bavarian ambassador, Grimm, who noted that both of the young people had developed greatly in the intervening years, but that audiences were less thrilled now that they were not so young. Nevertheless, they performed at Versailles and for the Princess of Orleans who presented young Wolfgang with a rondo that she had composed herself. They were also presented to Crown Prince Karl Wilhelm Ferdinand of Brunswick who had had such success during the Seven Years War. The Mozarts were very taken with this man because he was such an accomplished violinist, and very interested in Leopold's book on violin pedagogy. At this time, Mozart wrote a brief Kyrie for four-part chorus and orchestra, based on a French melody, which demonstrated his ability to absorb music around him and make it his own.

꧁꧂

They left Paris on July 9th and went south to Lyon and Dijon and then to the newly independent Geneva which was in turmoil. They then went to Lausanne, where they remained for several weeks at the insistence of Prince Ludwig of Württemberg. Thereafter, they went to Berne, and Zurich, where a concert of orchestral works was presented, until October 1766.

❧❧

They continued their Swiss sojourn and entered German lands, stopping at Donaueschingen, where they gave nine concerts in twelve days, to the great delight of the people. Here he also competed in the organ with the young virtuoso (two years his senior) Sixtus Bachmann and was deemed the winner.

❧❧

Then, they made their circuitous way to Munich by November 8th, where they performed for the Elector of Bavaria. The elector presented Mozart with a melody written in pencil, which Mozart turned instantly into a completed composition. However, despite his successes here, Wolfgang got sick, and they had to stay here longer than they had planned. By the end of November, though, they were home in Salzburg, having been gone for nearly four years. It was deemed a success because they were now well-known throughout Europe, but Leopold's main goal was not achieved. He wanted to get a permanent position for his son in one of the courts of Europe, and he had failed in that task. Accordingly, he set about planning another tour for the next year.

❧ IV ❧
SETBACKS AND SUCCESS IN VIENNA

"I am one of those who will go on doing till all doings are at an end."

— WOLFGANG AMADEUS MOZART

Almost as soon as he had arrived in Salzburg though, he was

asked to write a piece for the archbishop's ordination. This work's authorship was questioned by the archbishop, who locked Mozart in a room for a week and demanded that he write an oratorio. The resulting work, KV 35, was greatly acclaimed at its premiere, and the archbishop was assured of his genuine talent. In keeping with his newly admired abilities, he was commissioned to write a piece for the Jesuit school in Salzburg, which was performed in May 1767. A dramatic work called **Clementia Croesi** was performed with Mozart's **Apollo et Hyacinthus seu Hyacinthi Metamorphosis**.

⚜

On September 11th, 1767, the Mozart family went to Vienna, staying with a gold merchant, whose three children all came down with small pox. Fearing for his children's safety, on October 23rd, the entire family fled the city for Brno to escape the smallpox epidemic that had taken over the city. On October 26th, though, having left Brno, Mozart began to show signs of the deadly disease, while they were in Olmütz. Although Mozart went temporarily blind as a result of this, he recovered by November, at which time Nannerl came down with the disease. She too recovered though, and by the end of the year, they were ready to return to Vienna. The irony of this situation was that there was an inoculation available against smallpox, but Leopold chose not to inoculate his children, believing that it may harm their creativity.

⚜

The family set off for Vienna in December 1767, stopping in Brno for two weeks, at the invitation of the brother of the archbishop of Salzburg, arriving in Vienna on January 10th,

1768. Here they were presented to Empress Maria Theresa on January 19th, and she was clearly very glad to see them.

৩৯৪৩

In January 1768, Leopold Mozart took an offhand remark as a commission to write an opera and was disappointed when Wolfgang's first opera, *La finta semplice*, (KV 51) went unperformed. Things in Vienna were cut-throat though, and a series of silly intrigues from jealous composers meant that it was never performed there. Instead, his little music theatre work, an opera buffa in French ***Bastien et Bastienne***, composed when he was in France, was performed to great acclaim.

৩৯৪৩

In addition, Mozart was asked to write a mass, which resulted in his Mass in G major (KV 49), considered by many theorists as his first mature work.

❧ V ❧
THE SOLO TRIP
TO ITALY

"Neither a lofty degree of intelligence nor imagination nor both together go to the making of genius. Love, love, love, that is the soul of genius."

— WOLFGANG AMADEUS MOZART

PREPARATIONS

❧

L eopold felt strongly that, to be a complete musician, one had to go to Italy to study. It was a long tradition in German lands, from Hans Leo Hassler, Heinrich Schuetz, and Handel, that one needed to learn the style of the Italians.

❧

Dated September 30th, 1769, Leopold received a letter of recommendation from Johann Adolf Hasse, the dean of German Italianate music, addressed to Abbate Giovanni Maria Ortes in Bologna. It is a very flattering portrait of father and son, and although Leopold soon realized that concerts in Italy were always privately organized, unlike the practice in Austria and the German lands, and so remuneration would be in the form of some trinket or a small amount of money, rather than the admission he was used to charging.

Nevertheless, he felt that it was essential to organize this trip, and he went through with it. Just before they left, Wolfgang was appointed Konzertmeister to the archbishop.

FIRST SUCCESSES

꧁꧂

Leopold and Wolfgang set off for Italy on December 13th, 1769, leaving Anna Maria and Nannerl at home. Their first stop was Innsbruck where they were met by Count Johann Nepomuk Spaur, the brother of the Salzburg Cathedral canon. At a concert on the 15th, Mozart sight-read a concerto, which he received as a gift along with twelve ducats.

꧁꧂

They continued their journey on December 19th and stopped in the small Italian town of Rovereto, where Mozart was showered with gifts from the Italian noblemen who welcomed him. They played a concert at the home of Baron Giovanni Battista Todeschi which was so full that they needed to use bouncers to get to the organ through the standing-room-only crowd. Leopold thought with some evidence that if this were the welcome they were to receive in all of Italy, they would have a great deal of fame before the end of this sojourn.

❦

They continued to Verona where operas were being performed every night but Monday, making it difficult for the Mozarts to organize a concert. But when Wolfgang performed a symphony of his own composition and sight-read difficult music and extemporized an aria that he sang himself, the people of Verona went crazy. He saw an opera called **Ruggiero** with a libretto by Metastasio (composer unknown).

❦

He then went on to Mantua on January 10th, 1770, where it was cold but pleasant. On Mantua, he was widely admired, especially by the noble women of the town who wept when he left. He performed a concert on January 16th, 1770 and saw Hasse's **Demetrio** as well.

❦

The two of them went on to Cremona, the town where the great Stradivarius, Guarneri, and Amati violins were made. He also saw a performance of Hasse's (libretto by Metastasio) **La Clemenza di Tito** which he would later set to music himself.

MILAN

❦

They continued to the large center of northern Italy, Milan, where they were put up in the Augustine monastery of San Marco. Count Karl Joseph von Firmian, the governor general, was their host for most of the stay. They met the great opera composer Niccolò Piccinni whose opera *Cesare in Egitto* was being produced there. He was tested by the great sacred music composer, Giambattista Sammartini, who was very impressed with his abilities.

❦

When Mozart had thoroughly charmed the nobility of Milan, Count von Firmian commissioned an opera seria from Mozart to be performed at the Teatro Regio Ducal in Milan.

❦

After a number of concerts where he was well received, they

continued to Bologna, where Padre Martini and the great Carlo Broschi, known as Farinelli, who was already retired but enjoyed entertaining musicians at his villa. Farinelli had made an enormous success all over Europe, including Vienna, Spain, and London, and Mozart was very impressed with his singing even in his old age.

FLORENCE

❦

On March 30th, 1770, they arrived in Florence, which was the capital city of Tuscany, and thanks to letters of recommendation from Austrian nobles, they were warmly received by the Grand Duke Leopold and the Imperial ambassador, Count Rosenburg. Mozart was invited to play at court on April 2, accompanied by the great violinist Pietro Nardini, who also gave him difficult fugues to play. The director of music in Florence was the Marquis de Ligneville, and he also put Mozart to the test with complicated fugues for him to play, all of which he did almost effortlessly. Also, in Milan, he met the singer Giovanni Manzuoli who had been friends with them in England and learned that he had been approached by the Milanese authorities to perform in Mozart's new opera. He also met Thomas Linley, who was another child prodigy, a thirteen-year-old violinist. He and Mozart became good friends, and Linley suffered the sad fate of an early death when he drowned in a boating accident in 1778.

ROME

❧

Although they wanted to stay in Florence, they knew that they had to reach Rome by Holy Week to gain maximum attention, and so they set off in atrocious weather, where the inns were unwelcoming and filthy, and the many of the roads were impassable. However, they arrived in Rome on April 11th, to terrible thunderclaps that made them think the city was under siege.

❧

The Mozarts arrived just in time to hear the Allegri **Miserere**, a piece of great importance to the Sistine Chapel choir, performed only on the Wednesday and Friday of Holy Week, written for two choirs, one of four parts, the other of five parts, which come together in the end of the work to nine-part harmony. Mozart heard it twice and then went home to copy it's notes perfectly from memory, thus producing the first unauthorized copy of this closely guarded property of the Vatican. It is important to understand that this work is a nine-part motet which lasts for about twenty minutes. Granted, there are quite a few repeats in the piece, as it is constructed somewhat like a rondo (with a section that is repeated after a contrasting section, every few minutes), but this feat is both incredible and typical of the young Mozart. He was fourteen years old when he did this, and although he was not totally aware of the importance of the piece, even though he was told of its great significance and the importance of secrecy. Even so, he managed to recreate it despite the warning that it must not be shared with those who were not in the Sistine Chapel.

FURTHER TRAVELS IN ITALY

❦

The pair left Rome on May 8th and continued south toward Naples, another center of great Italian opera. They arrived in Naples on May 14th.

❦

Armed with their letters of recommendation, the Mozarts were soon giving a concert on 28th May and attended the first performance of Niccolò Jommelli's opera ***Armida abbandonata*** at the famous San Carlo theatre. Mozart was invited to write an opera for the next season of San Carlo, but he declined because of his prior commitment to Milan. Sadly, they were not invited to play at the royal court, so Leopold decided to leave Naples and return to Rome after visiting the tourist sites of Mount Vesuvius, the twin buried towns of Herculaneum and Pompeii, and the Roman baths at Baiae. They departed for Rome on June 25th.

❦

In Rome, Mozart was granted an audience with the Pope and was made a knight of the Order of the Golden Spur. They left Rome and made their way back to Bologna, arriving on July 20th. While they were there, Mozart received a libretto (significantly, it was not the libretto they had expected, Metastasio's **La Nitteti**, but **Mitridate, re di Ponto,** by Vittorio Cigna-Santi) after Giuseppe Parini's Italian translation of Jean Racine's play, Mithridate.

❦

Written after a close study of the opera *La Nitteti* by Josef Mysliveček who had befriended him in Milan, this opera was composed and prepared for production in Bologna when Mozart met Mysliveček, and it was largely composed when he was in Bologna, with (one assumes) some help from Mysliveček. Mozart learned a great deal about the composition of opera from his friend and even incorporated some of his musical motifs into his own opera.

❦

While composing this work, Mozart applied for membership to the Accademia Filarmonica in Bologna. On October 9th, 1770, Mozart sat for an exam to be a member. He was required to write a four-part piece for voices, and although he was given four hours for its composition, Mozart finished it in a half hour and was elected to the Accademia despite the requirement that he be twenty years of age.

❦

Then, on October 18th, the two of them returned to Milan on October 18th, where he finished composing and preparing the **Mitradate** arias, which he had to do with considerable consultation with the singers, who had a great deal of control over what they would sing.

❧

The opera was premiered at the Teatro Regio Ducal in Milan, on 26th December 1770, (at the Milan Carnival), under Mozart's direction. It was a great success and was performed twenty-one times despite doubts because of Mozart's youth – he was 14 at the time. Sadly, for musical history, it was not revived until the twentieth century, as the original score has been lost (but some copies of the manuscript have been recently rediscovered). The opera features virtuoso arias for the principal roles, but only two short ensembles, as was typical of the style at the time. There is a single suet at the end of Act II and a quintet finale.

❧

This success led to further opera commissions from Milan; in October 1771, he was commissioned to write **Ascanio in Alba** in 1771 and **Lucio Silla** in 1772.

❧

For the remainder of his tour, Mozart visited Venice and was well received by the nobility of that city. He saw many operas and performed for many private functions, as well as enjoying the Carnevale for which Venice was famous. The two of them setback for Salzburg, arriving on March 28th, with a new commission for an opera in Milan to be premiered during carnival 1773 (this was **Lucio Silla**, and the other opera, **Ascanio in Alba**, which began life as a serenata, morphed into an opera and was performed in Milan in 1771).

※

Leopold and Wolfgang returned to Salzburg in December 1771, after Mozart completed his symphony (KV 114) on the 30th and thereafter fell seriously ill. While they were away, Archbishop Siegmund Schrattenbach had died on December 16th after a prolonged illness, and his successor, the former Bishop of Gurk was not a popular choice. Mozart was asked to write an opera for the entry into the town of the new arch-bishop, which would happen the next year, in 1772. Mozart wrote a serenata, **Il sogno di Scipione** (KV 126) to a text by Metastasio (adapted to suit the situation in Salzburg).

※

During 1772, Mozart stayed in Salzburg, composing a symphony (KV 124) in February, and three in May (KV 128, 129, 130). In July and August, he wrote three more symphonies, (KV 132, 133, and 134). The new Archbishop made Mozart's appointment as Konzertmeister permanent, at a salary of 150 florins, which helped a great deal in his finances.

※

On October 24th, the two male Mozarts left for Milan, arriving on November 4th, and began to meet with the singers. The opera premiered on December 26th and was a success, despite some performance peculiarities, and Mozart was happy with the result. In January 1773, while waiting to see if Wolfgang had been appointed to a music position in Tuscany, Mozart wrote a series of "*Milanese*" string quartets (KV 155/134a - KV 160/159a) as well as the solo motet *Exsultate, jubilate*, KV 165, which he wrote for the star of his opera, Rauzzini. This piece is a brilliant sacred work that is still performed regularly today.

இ

Sadly, the appointment in Florence never materialized, and he only learned of this on February 27, causing Leopold to explain his long absence from Salzburg by claiming that he had severe rheumatism that prevented him from traveling. They departed Milan on March 4th and arrived in Salzburg nine days later, without an Italian appointment and in a state of depression because of this. Mozart never went back to Italy after this.

❧ VI ☙

SALZBURG TO VIENNA

"I cannot write poetically, for I am no poet. I cannot make fine artistic phrases that cast light and shadow, for I am no painter. I can neither by signs nor by pantomime express my thoughts and feelings, for I am no dancer; but I can by tones, for I am a musician."

— WOLFGANG AMADEUS MOZART

❦

After finally returning from Italy on March 13th, 1773, Mozart returned to his employment at the court of the Prince-Archbishop Hieronymus Colloredo. He took this opportunity to write a number of different works, including new symphonies, piano, and violin sonatas, more string quartets, masses, serenades, and even a few less significant operas. Between April and December 1775, Mozart began to write violin concertos and eventually wrote five, which were also the only violin concertos he ever wrote. The last three KV 216, KV 218, and KV 219, are now frequently performed.

❦

In 1776, he began writing piano concertos, culminating in the E-flat Piano Concerto KV 271 of early 1777, considered by critics to be a masterpiece of the genre and a securely mature work.

❦

It is impossible to take these musical developments out of context though, and Mozart was not happy in Salzburg. He had seen some of the greatest works of great Italian composers and felt that Salzburg, for all its opportunity, was a backwater. He continued to apply for positions in other, larger centers. Mozart wanted to write more operas, and there were few occasions to do this in Salzburg. To make things worse, the court theater closed in 1775, making these opportunities even rarer.

༺༻

To try to secure work, Mozart recognized that Vienna was his most likely destination, and he and his father set off on July 14th for the capital city of the Austrian Empire. He stayed until September 1773.

༺༻

Trying their best to gain some sort of permanent position, Mozart and his father found that he was at an uncomfortable stage in his development. He was seventeen years old - too old to be a child prodigy, and too young to be taken seriously as an adult. He managed to get an audience with Empress Maria Theresa on August 4th, but nothing came of it despite her kindness to him. Trying to gain employment, he befriended the first violinist Franz Griebich, of the Imperial string quartet that frequently played at court. Mozart wrote six string quartets, KV 168-172, influenced by the work of the famous composer Franz Joseph Haydn. These were the first quartets he had written that had four movements, and many of them included fugues (KV 168 and 173) in the final move- ment. Likewise, the first movement of KV 170, rather than being in the accepted sonata-allegro form, is a set of variations on a theme. He also wrote a set of variations based on court composer Antonio Salieri's aria from ***La fiera di Venezia***, which had recently achieved success in Vienna.

❧

The stay in Vienna was singularly unsuccessful for a young composer so used to adulation. The two of them left Vienna on September 24th and arrived home a few days later. The Prince, Archbishop, who had been ill for much of the summer (curtailing musical events as a result) had recovered by September, although he actually died in January of the next year, 1774.

❧

When they returned to Salzburg, Mozart completed two symphonies in quick succession: KV 182, which is well-written but not brilliant, completed on October 3rd, and the "***little***" G minor Symphony, KV 183, completed on October 5th, which is an acknowledged masterpiece. The reason for the importance of this work stems from the recent musical and artistic development referred to as ***Sturm und Drang*** (literally "***storm and stress***"), which became the precursor to the Romantic style later in the century. ***Sturm und Drang*** is a style largely associated with the music of Haydn at this time, and so it is assumed that Mozart fell under the spell of this most friendly and jovial of composers, although there is no historical evidence that he even met Haydn during his visit to Vienna.

❧

During his time in Salzburg, he was befriended by Joseph

Haydn's illustrious composer brother, Michael Haydn, who was also employed by the court. He was helped and influenced by this kind man and encouraged to write sacred music, including two masses, the first in F (KV 192), and the other in D, (KV 194).

❧❦❧

Haydn was influenced by the Viennese style espoused by Michael Haydn's brother but also by the very famous Mannheim school that produced such great early classical symphonies by Graun and Stamitz. Why Mozart wrote so many symphonies at this time is unclear, but it is clear that it stood him in good stead in years to come.

❧❦❧

Although his life in Salzburg seemed pedestrian compared to his earlier successes in Italy, he did receive a commission from Munich to write an opera for the 1775 carnival season. He went to Munich from December 6th, 1774 until March 1775, although his only material success there was a successful mounting of his opera *La finta giardiniera*. Almost as soon as he got there, he developed a toothache that forced the delay of the premiere from December 29th to January 5th. Sadly, because of problems with the singers, the opening was further delayed and finally opened on January 13th. Ironically, Antonio Tozzi, who had stolen the show the previous year with his successful opera buffa, was commissioned to write the opera seria which was eclipsed by Mozart's *La finta giardiniera*. Mozart was particularly happy because his sister Nannerl was there to witness his success.

❧❦❧

Back in Salzburg, after a successful run of his opera but without any permanent appointment, which both he and his father had been hoping for, he returned essentially empty-handed. And he began something new, something that would establish his reputation in years to come: he started writing solo piano sonatas. The first set of six piano sonatas, KV 279-284, were dedicated to Baron von Dürnitz, an amateur bassoonist and keyboard player who failed to pay Mozart for them. Still, they became staples of Mozart's later concerts in Mannheim and Paris.

❧

Similarly, many of his keyboard concertos, including the three-keyboard concerto (KV 242) were written for his students, who were often female members of the nobility of Salzburg and the surrounding areas.

❧ VII ❧
AUGSBURG, MANNHEIM, PARIS, AND MUNICH

"We live in this world in order always to learn industriously and to enlighten each other by means of discussion and to strive vigorously to promote the progress of science and the fine arts."

— WOLFGANG AMADEUS MOZART

❦

In August of 1777, Mozart requested another leave of absence from Archbishop Colloredo but was refused. In fact, the Archbishop was so annoyed at yet this request that he dismissed both Wolfgang and Leopold. He wrote:

> *"Father and son are granted permission to find their fortune elsewhere — in accordance with the Gospel."*

This, of course, put both of them in a difficult financial position, but nevertheless, on September 23rd, Mozart set out in search of permanent employment, visiting Munich, Augsburg, Mannheim, and Paris.

❦

Instead of going with his father, who needed to beg for his position at court again, his father decided that Wolfgang was to go with his mother. This was theoretically a good idea, but things went terribly wrong nonetheless.

❧

His first stop was Munich where he had had success a few years before. However, although he brought all the letters of recommendation he could find, and his knighthood from the Pope, as well as an offer to compose four operas for their next season, the Elector decided that he wanted Mozart to "**go to Italy**," suggesting that he did not know of Mozart's early success in Italy. Consequently, there were few opportunities for employment here. His main experience of note was his introduction to the idea of a German opera; after this, he became convinced that opera was suitable for the German language, and he longed to write an opera in German if he could secure a commission.

❧

While in Augsburg, he re-acquainted himself with his distant cousin, Maria Anna Thekla, whom he called "***Bäsle***." The two of them clearly got along, and possibly became lovers as his letter to her suggests:

> "I kiss your hands, your face, your knees, even your — in a word, anything you let me kiss!"

This weird event speaks to the growing adulthood that Mozart so relished and his father so feared.

❧

There were not many opportunities for him in either Munich or Augsburg, but he had made some connections while in Salzburg and Vienna with members of the most famous orchestra in Europe, the Mannheim orchestra, and many of them convinced him that he would do well in Mannheim.

MANNHEIM

✿

While he was in Mannheim in the fall of 1777, Mozart met and fell in love with Aloysia Weber, a singer from a musical family who had lived in Vienna and Mannheim, and the sister of the great German composer Carl Maria von Weber's father Franz.

✿

Johann Baptist Wendling, the principal flutist in the Mannheim orchestra, introduced Mozart to a wealthy amateur flutist named Ferdinand De Jean, who was a surgeon in the Dutch East India Company. Mozart had often adapted his musical compositions to suit a particular social or musical setting, and his father insisted that he accept all commissions, no matter how trivial or poorly paid. De Jean commissioned Mozart to write three easy flute concertos and two flute quartets, and although he famously hated the flute, he accepted. Mozart, it seems, absolutely loathed this man, but this only became stronger when this amateur decided to pay Mozart only half the money he had promised him. Nevertheless, Mozart completed a D-major quartet on December 25th, 1777, and scored the work, according to De Jean's wishes, in the manner of a string quartet.

ଊଃ୫

After this unfortunate experience, Mozart realized that there were few prospects for employment in Mannheim, though he set off with his mother to Paris on March 14th, 1778.

ଊଃ୫

While Mozart was in Paris, Aloysia was hired as a singer in Munich in the intervening time, and her whole family moved to Munich. When Mozart passed through Munich on his way back home, she rejected him, but he stayed in touch with the family, even after they moved to Vienna. He would later marry her younger sister, Constanze, when he moved into a room in the family home of the Webers in Vienna.

PARIS

☙❧

In Paris, Mozart found life very comfortable at first, staying with Ambassador Grimm. However, before long, they had a falling out, and Mozart and his mother were forced to stay at a seedy hotel. He began to fall into debt and started pawning his valuables. The fact was, Mozart was not fluent in French and lacked the push that his father had. His mother, terrified of foreign places, languished in a cold, unheated room, while Wolfgang went out to try to meet Marie Antoinette, the daughter of Maria Theresa, and wife of Louis XVI.

☙❧

As a result of these uncomfortable living conditions, Anna Maria Mozart's health began to fail, and when she refused treatment from French physicians, her condition became serious. On July 3rd, 1778, Mozart wrote a letter in great distress:

*"I have very painful and sad news to give you, which, in fact,
accounts for my not having replied sooner to your letter.
My dearest mother is very ill. They have bled her
according to custom, which was indeed quite necessary
and did her a lot of good. But a few days later she
complained of shivering and feverishness. As she became
worse by the minute, could barely speak, and lost her
hearing, we had to shout to her. Baron Grimm [the
Bavarian ambassador with whom he was staying] sent
his doctor to see her. She is still very weak, still feverish
and delirious. They do give me some hope, but I don't
have much. I wavered from hope to fear day and night,
but I'm completely reconciled to the will of God, and hope
that you and my sister will be too... Let us put aside these
sad thoughts, and still hope, but not too much... I have
written a symphony for the opening of the "**Concert
Spirituel**," which was performed to great applause on
Corpus Christi day. I was very nervous during the
rehearsal because in my whole life I've never heard
anything go so badly. You can have no idea of the way
they scraped and scurried through it twice. I was really
very edgy, and I would have been happy to have it
rehearsed again, but there wasn't time. So, I went to bed
with an aching heart, dissatisfied and angry. The next
day I decided not to go to the concert at all, but the fair
evening weather made me change my mind. I was,
nonetheless, determined that if the performance went as
badly as the rehearsal, I would go into the orchestra, take
the violin from the first violinist, and lead myself."*

෧෴෨

Unbeknownst to him at the time of writing, Anna Maria
Mozart would die that night. The "***Paris***" Symphony in D

major (KV 297) that he wrote for the Concert Spiruel. The world premiere took place on June 12th, 1778, in a private performance in the home of Count Karl Heinrich Joseph von Sickingen, the ambassador to the Electorate of the Palatinate. The public premiere took place six days on June 26th, 1778, at the Concert Spiruel and again on August 15th.

※※

Even at his time of terrible privation and sadness from the illness that would soon kill his mother, Mozart wrote an impressive symphony. It is scored for two flutes, two oboes, two clarinets in A, two bassoons, two French horns, two trumpets, timpani, and strings (twenty-two violins, five violas, eight 'cellos, and five basses. It was also Mozart's first symphony to use clarinets.

※※

It is also only in three movements, omitting the minuet and trio (third) movement, and the first movement begins with a rising motif that is typical of the Mannheim school. This effect, in combination with a huge crescendo, is called the Mannheim Rocket. As he wrote to his father, after having slammed his audiences and the orchestra:

> *"In the middle of the opening Allegro there was a passage that I knew people would like; the whole audience was carried away by it, and there was tremendous applause. But I knew when I wrote it what sort of an effect it would make, and so I introduced it again at the end, with the result that it was encored."*

Clearly Mozart knows by now how to impress an audience, and it succeeded, but many other factors also kept him from taking a position in France. He had thought at some point that a position as organist at Versailles which would have occupied him only half the year, and with a salary of two thousand livres, but he also said that he would not have accepted it. And, for the sake of history, that is a good thing, given the future of the royal family in France.

SONATA-ALLEGRO FORM

❦

Mozart was the great master of this form, the most malleable of all forms and the quintessentially Classical form. It grew out of several different forms that were current at the time. Mozart was preternaturally fond of the Mannheim school of playing and composing, repeatedly mentioning how much he wanted to work there. This was the school of Johann Stamitz, Jiri Antonin Benda, and Franz Xaver Richter, where the famous orchestra, whose virtuosic style is often referred to as the Mannheim Rocket (or Steamroller), wrote their symphonies that were so hugely influential to his developing style.

❦

Mozart absorbed these influences like a sponge and went on to create that is now considered the most sophisticated musical forms in the entire Classical repertoire. Sadly, his music may have been improving from the perspective of the modern-day listener, but not with the other Viennese composers around him, which is why he had such trouble getting a post at court (that and the fact that he was notoriously indiscreet and possibly even rude to people around him!).

⚜

Regardless, his form of communicating was the sonata form – a malleable and brilliant reflection of the new philosophy of the Enlightenment, similar to the new legal system (Common Law and, somewhat later, the Code Napoleon), where adversaries vie for supremacy, or in the scientific method (where a theory is put forward, put to the test, and, on the basis of the results, concluded) or indeed the brilliant Hegelian dialectic (in which two opposing discursive topics are presented, discussed and resolved). Sonatas tend to involve a number of subjects (musical melodies chord progressions, key areas, or other recognizable elements), which are presented (in the "***Exposition***"), which is stated twice for emphasis, then discussed (in the "***Development***" where they are bandied about in various keys, put together, and generally tested), and then resolved (in the "***Recapitulation***"). This system, which is so perfectly in tune with the Enlightenment, was perhaps a little ahead of its time, given the autocratic rule in the city, and the participation of the very people he wanted as patrons!

PARIS AGAIN

꩜

While Mozart was still in Paris, Leopold had been trying to get Mozart his position back again by telling the Archbishop of his great successes, and so the Archbishop agreed to reinstate Wolfgang to his position as Konzertmeister at a salary of five hundred florins. Leopold wrote to Wolfgang to tell him the good news, and that the young lady Aloysia Weber, whom he had fallen in love with, was not only to sing in the opera in Salzburg but to live in Leopold's house. All this news conspired to convince Mozart to return to Salzburg. And so, in the late fall of 1778, Mozart set out to return to Salzburg, stopping first in Strasbourg where he gave some concerts, and then moved to Mannheim. Mannheim had always been very fond of Mozart, and, in his own words "the way I love Mannheim, Mannheim loves me, too," he wrote his father. The only person who did not love him in Mannheim, it seems, was Aloysia Weber, who, when he met her there, made it clear that his love for her was not reciprocated. He did write a duodrama called

Semiramis, inspired by the great Mannheim composer Benda, which has sadly been lost.

☙❧

Mozart reached Salzburg in January 1779. During his year in Salzburg, he wrote a mass, which is a great work but not appreciated. He also probably wrote an opera called ***Zaide***, which is virtually forgotten today.

☙❧

In the fall of 1780, Mozart met a person who would one day be a very important collaborator. Emanuel Schikaneder had a German theatrical troupe that was based in Vienna, but who visited Salzburg that year. Schikaneder became a family friend of the Mozarts, and the Mozarts went to many of his shows. Eventually, Schikaneder would become the librettist for Mozart's brilliant German *Singspiel* (play with songs or, what we might today call a musical), ***The Magic Flute***.

❧ VIII ❧
MUNICH AND IDOMENEO

"I thank my God for graciously granting me the opportunity of learning that death is the key which unlocks the door to our true happiness."

— WOLFGANG AMADEUS MOZART

❧

It was in 1780 that Mozart finally received a commission from Munich: an opera seria on the subject of the king of Crete: **Idomeneo**. After three days in transit, Mozart arrived in Munich in November 1779, where he was given perfect working conditions, and he created what is generally considered to be his first mature opera. He had the incredible Mannheim orchestra to work with, and the world-class ensemble of singers in the employ of the Elector of Pfalz, Karl Theodor, at his disposal. He had already successfully collaborated with the theatre director, Joseph Count Seeau in Munich during the production of **La Finta Giardiniera**. The libretto was based on the tragedy **Idoménée** by Antoine Danchet but was reworked into Italian by the Salzburg court chaplain, Giambattista Varesco.

❧

Because Mozart had the greater fame than Varesco, he was able to exert great influence over the libretto. He was determined to break many of the accepted operatic rules to create something completely new and exciting.

☙❦❧

Idomeneo is a lyrical tragedy in the form of an opera seria with many effective new traits, like the increased instrumentation in the orchestra, and the much-increased use of the chorus. It is generally considered Mozart's greatest choral opera. He also exerted his influence on the dramaturgy, shortened parts to increase their effects, increased the suspense with a dense use of instruments and wrote the marvelous ballet music. The premiere in Munich in 1781 at the Residenz Theatre was a great success. In fact, so happy was Mozart after the premiere that he stayed three months and enjoyed the carnival season to the full. Only when the Archbishop of Salzburg summoned Mozart back to Salzburg, ending the most pleasant time in his life, Mozart left Munich.

✺ IX ✺
MOZART IN VIENNA

"How sad it is that these great gentlemen should believe what anyone tells them and do not choose to judge for themselves! But it is always so."

— WOLFGANG AMADEUS MOZART

∞∞

The Archbishop of Salzburg seems to have been hellbent on bringing Mozart's self-confidence to a manageable level and

was summoned to Vienna, where the court had moved, and his salary was reduced to 400 florins, and his seat at the table reduced to sitting with the cooks and other menial servants. When Mozart asked leave to give a concert in Vienna, the Archbishop refused him this request, and further, when he asked to have leave to attend a concert with the Countess of Thun in order to gain an audience with Emperor Joseph II, it was also refused. As a result, Mozart quit, giving up his salary and his residence, and found a place to live in Vienna with the Weber family, who had begun taking in boarders since Fridolin, the father, had died. To supplement what little income he had from commissions, he began to give lessons in piano.

⚜

Leopold had decided that, to keep his position in the court of Salzburg, he would side with the Archbishop in this argument, and as a result, Mozart temporarily lost touch with his father. This must have been a blow to him as he had recently lost his mother as well.

⚜

Mozart was introduced to the great keyboard works of Johann Sebastian Bach, and particularly the forty-eight preludes and fugues called *The Well-Tempered Clavier*, by the generous patron of the arts Baron Gottfried von Swieten (1733-1803).

⚜

Mozart was continually looking for work and commissions,

and permanent appointments from nobles, but nothing was forthcoming. He began work on his escape opera, **_The Abduction from the Seraglio_** in September on 1781, but owing to many hindrances in its production, he gave up on it for the time.

CONSTANZE WEBER

Although things were not going well professionally for Mozart, he had begun to court Constanze Weber, the younger daughter of his erstwhile love, Aloysia Weber, who was now living in Vienna with her family. When Leopold heard about this romance, he wrote to Wolfgang to insist that he ended things between them as he felt it would hurt his career. Mozart wrote back to reassure his father that nothing was going on, and even moved out of Weber's house to quash the rumors. Still, by December, he wrote back to his father to ask his blessing for the union which his father reluctantly granted, although his father never accepted this marriage and held it against Wolfgang until his own death in 1787. Nevertheless, things progressed rapidly between the two lovers, and in 1782, on August 4th, they were married, shortly after his first successful production of an opera in Vienna. Mozart and Constanze were very happily married, and they had six children together, two of whom survived to adulthood. Poverty began to dog them in the latter days of their married life, but happiness also seemed to follow them. Rarely in musical history has any marriage been so happy. They shared a love of and a talent for music, and Constanze was a devoted and fun-loving wife to a fun-loving Mozart. When they visited Salzburg the next year, she sang the soprano solo for his *Mass in C Minor*, KV 427.

THE ABDUCTION FROM THE
SERAGLIO

꧁꧂

Mozart's first great German opera, ***The Abduction from the Seraglio***, was premiered on July 16th, 1782, and the Vienna Burgtheater.

꧁꧂

Joseph II had created a project called the **Nationalsingspiel**, or National sung theater, to counter the fad of Italian opera that had had a stranglehold over this fundamentally German-speaking city. Mozart's opera was the first production of this new entity headed by Gottfried Stephanie, who became the librettist. In fact, this opera was, other than some notable translations of Italian operas, the only successful project to come from this project, which was ultimately abandoned as a failure.

꧁꧂

Mozart wrote this opera incredibly quickly, believing that he only had two months to write the entire thing. However, he was granted a reprieve when they substituted a Gluck opera for the occasion it was originally intended, and Mozart's opera was to be performed the next summer. He wrote to his father about of his thoughts on the importance of the composer and librettist (writer of the words). In a letter he wrote to his father dated October 13th, 1781, he said

> "I would say that in an opera, the poetry must be altogether an obedient child to the music. Why are Italian comic operas popular everywhere – in spite of their miserable librettos? It is because the music reigns supreme, and when you listen to it, everything else is forgotten. An opera is a guaranteed success when the plot is well worked out, the words written only for the music and not shoehorned in here or there to suit some terrible rhyme. The best thing of all is when a good composer, who understands the theater and is talented enough to make sound judgments, meets a capable poet, that true phoenix; when this happens, nobody needs to worry about the applause, even from the ignorant."

۞

Mozart's thoughts on the role of the librettist are significant because, since its creation in 1600, opera gave pride of place to the libretto. The authors of the librettos were often noblemen, whereas in many cases, the composers were considered servants to these noblemen, and even great composers like Monteverdi or Cavalli would be treated terribly, their music replaced by the music of another composer, whereas the words were sacred territory. The librettists would sell their poetry at the operas, but the composers were sometimes not even credited at all. It took a person with the reputation and the genius of Mozart to assert the importance of the music to change this disproportionate importance on the libretto to the detriment of the music.

༺༻

For many years, Mozart had written a form of music now largely overlooked - the divertimento. He was able to secure a position in the court of the Emperor, but it was not the prestigious position he had wanted. Instead, he was in charge of writing garden music for the royal court, and so he set to work writing these rambling and often repetitive pieces, although they had his mark of genius too. In his first year alone on this job, he wrote two serenades and a divertimento for wind instruments, another serenade for two oboes, two clarinets and two bassoons, a symphony in D, and two concertos. He was less prolific in this year because he had to teach music to students every morning for a living. This life of the free musician has often been seen as a wonderful freedom and given a romantic tinge by authors who did not have to experience privation, but both Mozart and Beethoven were almost constantly in search of a patron, despite the increasingly obvious fact that the age of patronage was swiftly ending.

MOZART AND HAYDN

In 1784, Mozart finally met Joseph Haydn the great symphonist and wannabe opera composer, and they quickly became friendly. Although Haydn was still occupied most of the year in Esterhaza, the country estate of a very rich Hungarian nobleman, when he was in Vienna, he could seek Mozart out, and they would perform each other's string quartets. Haydn's six opus 20 string quartets from 1772, referred to as the "**Sun Quartets**" were widely seen as the inspiration for Mozart's 1773 KV 168-173 quartets that he wrote in Vienna. They probably first met face to face at a concert in which both of their music was being performed, on December 22nd and 23rd, 1783. Haydn was fifty-two and the most famous composer in Europe at the time, while Mozart was a young man whose opera ***The Abduction from the Seraglio*** had premiered to great success in Vienna and was now being performed in several European cities.

☙❧

The thing that brought them together was their mutual love for the medium of the string quartet, which both of them wrote. They also put together a quartet in which Haydn played the first violin, the great opera composer Carl Ditters von Dittersdorf played the second violin, Mozart played viola, and the composer Vanhal played 'cello. Mozart dedicated six of his quartets (Mozart's "***Haydn***" quartets (KV 387, KV 421, KV 428, KV 458, KV 464 and KV 465), published in 1785, to Haydn in response to Haydn's Opus 33 from 1781. Dedication to another composer was unusual at the time, as was the dedication he attached to the work:

> *"A father, who had decided to send his sons out into the world, thought it as his duty to entrust them to the protection and guidance of a man who was very celebrated at the time, and who happened more importantly to be his best friend. In the same way, I send my six sons to you [...] Please then, receive them kindly and be to them a father,*

guide, and friend! [...] I beg you, though, to be indulgent
to those faults which may have escaped a father's partial
eye, and in spite of them, to continue your generous
friendship towards one who so highly appreciates it."

෨෪෨

Although at this time, Mozart was very successful, living well in expensive places, sending his children to expensive private schools, he had many detractors, and it is worth noting that Haydn acted nobly and as sort of a mentor to Mozart, helping him in his career. He once said of Mozart: "If only I could impress Mozart's incomparable works on the soul of every friend of music, and the souls of nobles in particular, as deeply, with the same musical understanding and with the same deep feeling, as I understand and feel them, the nations would vie with each other to possess such a jewel." Mozart, for his part, was very fond of Haydn and extremely impressed with his talent.

FREELANCE MUSICIAN

❧

From 1782 to 1785 Mozart began something that would later become a staple for independent musicians: he mounted concerts with himself as a soloist, presenting three or four new piano concertos each season. For his first such concert, he wrote his B-flat piano concerto and completed it only two days before the concert. Since space in theaters was scarce in Vienna, he sometimes booked peculiar venues: one time he mounted a concert in a large room in an apartment building called the Trattnerhof, and another time, he rented the ballroom of the Mehlgrube (a restaurant). These concerts became very popular, and the concertos he premiered at them are still fixtures of the repertoire.

❧

He earned large sums from these public concerts, and Mozart and his wife began to live a lavish lifestyle. They moved from their humble home to an expensive apartment, with a rent of 460 florins per year. Mozart also bought an expensive fortepiano (an early version of a pianoforte, that had a particularly hard action, and pedals operated by the knees) from Anton Walter for nine hundred florins, and a beautiful billiard table for about three hundred florins. The Mozarts sent their son Karl Thomas to an exclusive boarding school and hired a number of servants. Typical of Mozart's life, he never gave any thought to saving money, and this brief period of financial stability made his time of privation, his final years, all the more difficult to endure. He lived in a lavish apartment on Schulerstrasse, right behind St Stephen's Cathedral for 460 gulders a year, which was more than his father Leopold's yearly salary for working for the Archbishop of Salzburg.

MOZART'S CHILDREN

❧

❧

Mozart and Constanze Weber had their first child, Raimund
Leopold on June 17th, 1783, but by August 19th, he had died.
Undeterred by this personal tragedy, the two of them had a

further five children: Karl Thomas, who was born on September 21st, 1784, (who lived a long life with many interesting careers, none of which was in music until 1858), Johann Thomas Leopold who was born on October 18th, 1786, but died on November 15th of that year. Their first daughter, Theresia Constanzia Adelheid Friedericke Maria Anna who was both on December 27th, 1787, and lived only until June 29th, 1788, and Anna Maria, who was born on November 16th, 1789, but died later that day.

෪

The youngest son of Wolfgang and Constanze was Franz Xaver Wolfgang who was born on July 26th, 1791, and made a career, traveling through Europe and playing his father's music, advertising himself as Wolfgang Amadeus Mozart Junior. He was a good composer, with solid credentials, having studied with Hummel and Salieri and even Beethoven. Although he had a successful career even as a composer, he never ascended to the heights of his father and never escaped the huge shadow of his father either. He died in 1844.

෪

It was in 1784 that Mozart began to keep a record book of his compositions, with the date of composition for each. Some of these works were written with incredible haste. For example, he wrote the Sonata in B-flat for violin and piano (KV 454) for the female virtuoso violinist Regina Strinasacchi, but only completely notated the violin part. Nevertheless, he extemporized the piano part with little effort.

LEOPOLD'S LAST VISIT

৩৵৩

When Mozart's father finally came for a visit in 1785, things were still going quite well for him professionally. The Viennese publisher, Artaria, published his Haydn string quartets for one hundred ducats. Mozart's success as a freelance performing artist was now firmly established, and in a way that was unique for the time. He composed all his own music, and his concerts were well attended, but inevitably, the novelty wore off. He was still able to support himself with his concerts and with the odd (and increasingly rare) commission. He was forced several times to move to less lavish quarters, farther from the center of town. His marriage to Constanze Weber was part of the problem; always a profligate spender, she was even worse than he was, according to reports from the time. In ten years, they moved eleven times, each time to a place less luxurious.

❧ X ❧
MATURE STYLE 1786-90

"My Constanze is the virtuous, honourable, discreet, and faithful darling of her honest and kindly-disposed Mozart."

— WOLFGANG AMADEUS MOZART

Despite the great success of *The Abduction from the*

Seraglio, Mozart did relatively little operatic writing for the next four years, producing only a handful of unfinished works and the one-act Singspiel called *Der Schauspieldirektor*. He focused instead on his career as a piano soloist and writer of concertos. Around the end of 1785, Mozart moved away from keyboard writing and began his famous operatic collaboration with the librettist Lorenzo Da Ponte.

❦

Lorenzo Da Ponte (born Emanuele Conegliano on March 10th, 1749 – August 17th, 1838) was an Italian-born, and later American opera librettist, poet, and Roman Catholic priest. He wrote the libretti for twenty-eight operas by eleven different composers, including three of Mozart's most celebrated operas, *Don Giovanni* (1786), *The Marriage of Figaro* (1787), and *Così fan tutte* (1790).

❦

Born Jewish, he converted to Roman Catholicism with his family in 1864, so his father could marry a Jewish woman. In 1770, da Ponte took minor orders as a priest and became a professor of literature. Although he was a priest, he seems to have lived a fairly unconventional life, taking a mistress and fathering two children with her. In 1779, he was charged with indecency because of this (and because he was living in a brothel and organizing entertainments for the brothel) and banished from Venice for fifteen years. In 1781, he moved to a small town in Austria and later to Dresden where he used his connections within the nobility to get a letter of introduction to the Imperial Court Composer, Antonio Salieri. This connection led to his appointment as librettist for the Italian theatre in Vienna, and he also came under the patronage of the banker Raimund Wetzlar von Plankenstern, who was also a benefactor to Mozart.

⚜

Interestingly, Mozart and da Ponte got along very well, and although his first two operas with Mozart were intended for Mozart, his third, **Così fan tutte** was begun with Salieri but completed by Mozart, causing animosity between the two composers.

⚜

In 1790, when Emperor Joseph II died, da Ponte lost his patronage and moved to Paris, where the revolution was in full swing. He moved to London with his mistress with whom he had four more children, and later on to America, where he settled in New Jersey as a greengrocer. Later, he founded the New York Opera Company, which eventually became the Metropolitan Opera Company, and became a naturalized American citizen.

⚜

The first collaboration between Mozart and da Ponte was **The Marriage of Figaro**, based on one of three plays in a set by the French playwright Beaumarchais called **La folle journée, ou le Mariage de Figaro (The Mad Day, or The Marriage of Figaro)**. It was originally intended as a critique of a French law called the droit de seigneur, in which the lord of a land had the right to bed any bride granted the right to marry within his lands. In his preface to the libretto, da Ponte wrote:

"I have not made a translation, but rather an imitation, or let us say an extract.... I was compelled to reduce the sixteen original characters to eleven, two of which can be played by a single actor and to omit, in addition to one whole act, many effective scenes.... In spite, however, of all the zeal and care on the part of both the composer and myself to be brief, the opera will not be one of the shortest.... Our excuse will be the variety of development of this drama ... to paint faithfully and in full color the various passions that are aroused, and ... to offer a new type of spectacle...."

⚜

To be fair, he delivered on this promise. It premiered at the Burgtheater in Vienna on 1st May 1786. It tells how the servants Figaro and Susanna succeed in getting married, foiling the efforts of their philandering employer Count Almaviva to seduce Susanna and teaching him a lesson in fidelity. The fact that Mozart and da Ponte worked closely and well together was what produced a brilliant music drama unlike anything the world had ever seen, and which caused operas to be more highly regarded, and the death of the style of opera called opera seria, to wither and die by contrast.

⚜

Although the play was first presented in Vienna in 1784, it was quickly banned because it contained much that was offensive to the nobility and royal family, but Lorenzo da Ponte managed to get official permission to set it as an opera. Mozart was the person who selected this play as his subject and brought it to da Ponte. Da Ponte, in turn, turned it into the brilliant libretto that it is today, in six weeks. His major change, to appease the censors, was the replacement of

Figaro's climactic speech against inherited nobility with an equally angry aria against unfaithful wives. Despite widespread rumors to the contrary, the libretto was actually approved by the Emperor before Mozart wrote a note. It received nine initial performances, and the audience reaction was so positive that they had to repeat virtually every set piece. This became such an issue that the Emperor issued a decree that henceforth only solos could be repeated, and he posted a notice to that effect at the Burgtheater.

☙❦❧

The review in the ***Wiener Realzeitung*** was lavish in its praise:

> *"Mozart's music was generally admired by connoisseurs already at the first performance, if I except only those whose self-love and conceit will not allow them to find merit in anything not written by themselves. The public, however ... did not really know on the first day where it stood. It heard many a bravo from unbiased connoisseurs, but obstreperous louts in the uppermost story exerted their hired lungs with all their might to deafen singers and audience alike with their St! and Pst; and consequently, opinions were divided at the end of the piece. [This comment is referring to the paid claques that tried to disrupt the opera. It is unknown which composer paid them though.] Apart from that, it is true that the first performance was none of the best, owing to the difficulties of the composition. But now, after several performances, one would be subscribing either to the cabal or to the tastelessness if one were to maintain that Herr Mozart's music is anything but a masterpiece of art. It contains so many beauties, and such a wealth of*

ideas, as can be drawn only from the source of innate genius."

❧

The orchestra for *The Marriage of Figaro* is unusually large for the time: scored for two flutes, two oboes, two clarinets, two bassoons, two horns, two trumpets, timpani, and strings; the recitatives are accompanied by a keyboard instrument, usually a fortepiano or a harpsichord, with the bassline covered by a 'cello. It is about three hours long, quite a bit longer than operas of the time usually lasted.

❧

Although **The Marriage of Figaro** seems to have been relatively successful in Vienna, the premiere in Prague, the second city of Austria was much warmer, and it was a runaway success there, leading to a second collaboration the next year. The result of this collaboration was **Don Giovanni**, which was premiered in Prague in October of 1787 to great acclaim, but with less success in (again) Vienna in 1788.

❧

Interestingly, considering the subject matter of **Don Giovanni** (many people believe that the Commendatore is a sort of reference to the role Leopold played in Mozart's life,) Mozart's father died on May 28th, 1787.

❧

Mozart was also appointed "**chamber composer**" to Emperor

Joseph II in December 1787, after the death of the composer Gluck, who had held this position. It was only a part-time appointment, paying 800 florins per year, and required Mozart only to compose dances for the annual balls in the Redoutensaal. This income though, modest as it was, became important to Mozart when hard times arrived. According to the court records, this appointment was intended to ensure that Mozart did not leave Vienna for better and more lucrative work.

⚬⚭⚬

Also, in 1787, the young Ludwig van Beethoven spent several weeks in Vienna, hoping to study with Mozart. Although no reliable records survive to indicate whether the two composers ever met, the two composers certainly knew of each other's existence, and it is likely that Beethoven would have sought out Mozart, especially since he was studying with Haydn, and was not happy.

DON GIOVANNI

꧁꧂

Don Giovanni **or** il dissoluto punito ("**The Libertine Punished**") is a two-act opera with an Italian libretto by Lorenzo Da Ponte. It is based on the legends of Don Juan, a fictional libertine and seducer. It was also partly based on the famous Venetian adventurer and lover Giovanni Casanova who was a friend and colleague of Lorenzo da Ponte when he lived in Venice.

꧁꧂

The Prague Italian opera premiered it at the National Theater (of Bohemia), now called the Estates Theatre, on 29 October 1787. Da Ponte's libretto was billed as a dramma giocoso, a common designation of its time that denotes a mixing of serious and comic action. Mozart, though, entered the work into his catalog as an opera buffa. Although sometimes classified as comic, it blends comedy, melodrama, and supernatural elements.

❧❧❧

It was planned to be premiered in Prague to capitalize on the success of *The Marriage of Figaro* in that town and to celebrate a visit from Duchess Maria Theresa of Austria, the niece of Emperor, Joseph II, and her husband on October 14th, 1787. But the opera was not completed in time, and *The Marriage of Figaro* was substituted, and the premiered took place a month later. It was completed on the 28th or 29th of October. The overture, one of the greatest in all opera, was completed either the day before the premiere or on the very day of the performance.

❧❧❧

Scored for two flutes, two oboes, two clarinets, and two bassoons as well as two horns, two trumpets, three trombones (including alto, tenor, bass), timpani, basso continuo for the recitatives, and strings. The composer also specified occasional special musical effects, such as, during the ballroom scene at the end of Act I, two onstage ensembles to play dance music in synchronization with the orchestra. Each of these groups plays in its own meter (a 3/4 minuet, a 2/4 contredanse, and a fast 3/8 peasant dance), accompanying the dancing of the main characters. This tour de force of genius is one of the most incredible feats in all the music, and yet it is so subtle and so well-wrought that it does not immediately strike the listener are complex; instead, it is a subtle statement on the positions of each character in the drama and their place within the society of the opera. Don Giovanni is a nobleman (well, an ignoble nobleman, given that the first scene when we meet him he is running away from a sexual assault on Donna Anna) and so he dances the elegant and aristocratic minuet, while Zerlina, the peasant girl dances the beautiful but rustic contredanse, and her beau, Masetto dances the rustic ⅜ peasant dance.

☙❧

Another musical masterpiece is the serenade he sings, accompanied by a guitar, with pizzicato strings accompanying. Later, two of the interventions of the Commendatore ("*Di rider finirai pria dell'aurora*" and "*Ribaldo, audace, lascia a' morti la pace*") are accompanied by oboes, clarinets, bassoons, and trombones (with 'cellos and basses), producing a chilling effect.

☙❧

The opera was premiered on October 29th, 1787, in Prague under its full title of **Il dissoluto punito ossia il Don Giovanni** – Dramma giocoso in due atti (The Dissolute punished, or Don Giovanni, a comic drama in two acts). The work was incredibly successful, with audiences applauding and swooning. It was becoming clear to Mozart that, while there were all kinds of intrigue holding him back in Vienna, he was adored in Prague. The review in the **Prager Oberpostamtzeitung** read,

> "*Connoisseurs and musicians say that Prague has never heard anything like this,*"

and, on the other hand:

> "*the opera ... is extremely difficult to perform.*"

Lorenzo da Ponte was not at the opening, and so Mozart, who conducted from the keyboard, took all the accolades.

⚜

When it was presented in Vienna, the ending of the opera, in which the surviving cast members sing about how much they miss Don Giovanni after he is dragged down to hell by the Commendatore who attempts to drag him to hell, had to be cut. The moralistic nature of the Viennese audiences was not like the joy in Don Giovanni's antics that the Prague audiences enjoyed.

⚜

The opera was premiered in Vienna on May 7th, 1788. Mozart wrote two new arias - Don Ottavio's aria *"Dalla sua pace"* ("From his peace" KV 540a, composed on April 24th for the tenor Francesco Morella), and Donna Elvira's aria *"In quali eccessi ... Mi tradì quell'alma ingrata"* (*"What excesses ... He betrayed me that ungrateful soul"*, KV 540c, composed on 30 April for the soprano Caterina Cavalieri) – and the duet between Leporello and Zerlina *"Per queste tue manine"* (*"For these your little hands"* KV 540b, composed on 28 April). He also made some cuts in the Finale to make it shorter, particularly the section where Donna Anna and Ottavio, Donna Elvira, Zerlina, Masetto, and Leporello revealed their plans for the future (*"Or che tutti, o mio tesoro"* *"Now that all, my treasure"*). In order to connect *"Ah, certo è l'ombra che l'incontrò"* (*"It must have been the ghost she met"*) to the *"moral"* of the story *"Questo è il fin di chi fa mal"* (*"This is the end which befalls to evil-doers"*), Mozart composed a different version of *"Resti dunque quel birbon fra Proserpina e Pluton!"* (*"So, the wretch can stay down there with Proserpina and Pluto!"*). These cuts are very seldom performed in theatres today.

AFTER DON GIOVANNI

❦

After ***Don Giovanni***, despite the huge success of the opera, Mozart met one setback after another in his life. His inability to secure a good job at the Imperial Court was partly responsible for the fact that he was less and less in demand as a composer. For example, one of his concerts in 1790 had to be canceled simply because he could not sell enough subscriptions. His last three symphonies (39, 40, and 41) which are now justly regarded as his greatest symphonic works were written for a concert in 1788 that appears not to have taken place.

❦

The summer of 1788 was a terrible time for Mozart. Not only was he still grieving his father's death, and the death of his first daughter Theresia, but he also was terribly in debt, thanks to profligate spending by him and Constanze. Mozart was forced to write to his friend Michael Puchberg, to beg for a loan. Puchberg did help him out, but Mozart was still in desperate straits and never regained the financial stability of his earlier years.

SYMPHONY #40 IN G MINOR

❧

Mozart wrote his last three symphonies in a period of seven weeks in the summer of 1788. The second of the three, Symphony in G Minor, No. 40, is sometimes referred to as the "***Great***" G minor symphony, to distinguish it from the "***Little***" G minor symphony, No. 25. The two are the only minor-key symphonies Mozart wrote, with the possible exception of an early and recently rediscovered A minor symphony known today as the Odense Symphony. This is probably the best-known work by Mozart in the symphonic genre – although interestingly, the first movement is best known (the second is virtually ignored), followed by the final movement, which is so exciting that it practically pops off the page. The third movement, the minuet, and trio are so different from what Mozart usually does that they are also remarkable, but the second movement is sort of forgotten.

❧

The Austrian Empire had entered a war with Turkey, causing people to think of things other than music. On a personal level, Mozart's six-month-old daughter Theresia had just died, throwing him and his family into deep sadness.

❀❀❀

Mozart was typically a craftsman who wrote on commission. There was no commission for these works, and yet they are large, well-crafted (actually the autograph is full of little errors, but the musical work is excellent), and substantial pieces.

❀❀❀

He may have been trying to build up a body of new work that he could use for subscription concerts. The problem with this theory is that he never seems to have actually played them. It is likely that his old friend Antonio Salieri may have performed at least this symphony at a subscription concert in 1789. Another possibility is that Mozart was hoping to be invited to England, as Haydn had been. He had wowed audiences and aristocrats while he was there as a child. Haydn had been approached by Salomon to tour to London, the financial (and, increasingly, the artistic) capital of Europe, and Mozart clearly had a similar plan in mind. He may have written this symphony along with the other two (39 and 41) so that he could present them when he went to England. Of course, he did not live to see that happen, although the key of G minor was a key that the great English composer, Johann Christian Bach, with whom Mozart had studied while in London, favored. His minuet is highly contrapuntal and complex, (one might say "*artificial*" in the old-fashioned sense of the term) and is clearly a theoretical minuet more than a genuine, danceable one. In fact, given the history of the minuet, it is one of the saddest and most tragic-sounding minuets ever written. It is astounding how it builds and builds to a brilliant contrapuntal climax though.

❧

He may – this is the least likely but most attractive of the options – simply have been compelled to express himself. Mozart's fortunes had dwindled to such an extent that he was forced to move to the suburbs of Vienna because of his financial woes, and with the loss of his daughter, the economic downturn due to the war, and his own loss of "popularity," may have put him into a funk, and the G minor symphony, in particular, is very sad.

❧

G minor is not a key that Mozart favored. The best supporting evidence for this theory is the formal qualities of the work itself – three of the four movements are – uncharacteristically – in sonata-allegro form. The first movement is, of course, but the finale is also a sonata, as is the tragic second movement.

❧

The first movement starts with an accompaniment figure and quickly provides the main theme, the main quasi-baroque theme, filled with descending minor second "*sighing*" motifs. The second subject is much more melodic, sadder, but it seems to talk itself out of a bad mood very quickly. The first subject is bandied about even in the first section. The development section contains enharmonic and chromatic writing, which begins with the first-group material in F minor. Listening to the development section, one is reminded of Mozart's love for Bach and his contrapuntal intricacies – something he learned from London Bach (Johann Christian), and something that he surely knew would be popular in London. It feels like a genuine tribute to his favorite long-dead composer.

⚝

The Andante (second movement) is not written in the normal style of second movements. There is no long aria-like melody. It is restless. Listen to the first 35 seconds, and you will get a sense of a composer working out a melody, rather than stating one. It seems to discuss itself. Strangely, the two subjects are complementary – like sonata form. In fact, this movement is a sonata too.

⚝

The minuet and trio are so contrapuntal as very nearly to defy the title. The incremental build of the minuet is overwhelmingly dramatic, in a Mannheim Rocket sort of way. Contrasted with the trio, which is gentle and pretty, working out the winds in a truly calming way, it seems tailor-made for English audiences of the late 18th century.

⚝

The finale, the third sonata in this work, is another rocket. It attacks you in a really un-Classical way. As wild as the opening is, it cannot be compared with the development section, which begins with a flourish intended to disorient any tonally-minded listener. He tosses off diminished chords with wild abandon. Then, he throws us whole-hog into a four-part contrapuntal working out of the material. The breathlessness of this movement must be a giant thrill to conduct. The weird clarinet writing (an afterthought for Mozart and held up as proof that he must have had a performance if he were to write a part for the clarinets) is very original.

❧

Strangely, Mozart has no timpani and no trumpet in this most bombastic of works. This points to the theory that he had a particular orchestra (maybe an English one, maybe a memory of the Mannheim one that was predominantly strings with a tiny number of winds and brass).

❧

The effect we are left with is a piece of profoundly moving proportions – this is only one of two symphonies Mozart wrote in G minor – or, for that matter, in any minor key. It has many aspects of the composer's mind embedded in its choice of instrumental groupings, its formal construction, its key, its quasi-baroque material, and its contrapuntal treatment. It is a remarkable work that is widely admired about ten years too late.

❧

At the time he was writing this work, Mozart was troubled by a lack of commissions, and by the recent death of his six-month-old daughter, Theresia. One letter to a lodge brother refers to *__dark thoughts which I must banish by force,__* and apparently those thoughts interfered in his ability to compose. During this summer, Mozart completed very few compositions. The only significant works were three symphonies, written in a mere seven weeks. They would be the final symphonies of his career.

❧ XI ❧
MOZART'S FINAL DAYS

«Believe me, I do not like idleness but work.»
Wolfgang Amadeus Mozart

In 1789, he traveled to Dresden, where he performed on the organ the Bach had used at the Thomaskirche, and then to Berlin. He did receive a commission for an opera from Emperor Joseph II, and once again he chose Lorenzo da Ponte to write the libretto. Although Cosi fan tutte was a brilliant work, filled with hilarity and musical ingenuity, it was performed only five times when the Emperor died in February 1790. A period of mourning took place which put the show on hold, costing Mozart a great deal.

༖

Così fan tutte, ossia La scuola degli amanti ("***Thus do all women or The School for Lovers***") KV 588, is an Italian-language opera buffa in two acts by Wolfgang Amadeus Mozart first performed on 26th, January 1790 at the Burgtheater in Vienna, Austria. The libretto was written by Lorenzo Da Ponte. Antonio Salieri tried to set the libretto but left it unfinished.

༖

Mozart's last great opera was actually what one might call a musical today: ***The Magic Flute*** occupied much of Mozart's time in the first half of 1791, in collaboration with his friend and fellow Freemason, Emanuel Schikaneder. In July, according to legend, Mozart was visited by a mysterious stranger who was bearing a commission, for a hefty fee, of a funeral mass called a *Requiem*. Mozart was not well, and in his illness, became convinced that this mass was to be for his own funeral. Then, he was interrupted again with a commission to write an opera for the coronation of Emperor Leopold II as King of Bohemia (in Prague). This commission was to be a re-setting of Metastasio's oft-composed libretto *La **Clemenza di Tito***, and he wrote the opera in little more than two weeks. To do this, Mozart hired his student Franz Xavier Süssmayr to compose the recitatives. This opera was an opera seria that Mozart himself did not favor, and it was only a moderate success, but it definitely caused Mozart to get even sicker. Then he had to return to finish ***The Magic Flute*** which was performed in Vienna on September 30th, less than a month after ***La Clemenza di Tito***.

৪৩৪

Mozart died on December 5th, 1791, a few weeks before his thirty-sixth birthday, leaving the ***Requiem*** unfinished. He was buried in a common grave, as was the contemporary Viennese custom, at the St. Marx Cemetery outside the city on December 7th. Salieri, Süssmayr, van Swieten, and two other musicians were present, although it was customary at the time not to have mourners. The legend that he was buried during a blinding snowstorm is not true; the day was calm and mild.

❧ XII ☙

MOZART'S PLACE IN THE WORLD OF MUSIC

"When I am traveling in a carriage, or walking after a good meal, or during the night when I cannot sleep; it is on such occasions that ideas flow best and most abundantly."

— WOLFGANG AMADEUS MOZART

Mozart is one of the most remarkable artists to have appeared on earth in any field. He seemed able to write music, complete and perfect, down to the last accent and inflection, with almost no thought. He is the most prolific composer ever to have lived, given the number of years he had to compose. He composed over six hundred different works, including twenty-one stage and opera works, fifteen Masses, forty-one symphonies, twenty-five piano concertos, twelve violin concertos, twenty-seven concert arias, seventeen piano sonatas, and twenty-six string quartets, not to mention the dance music, divertimentos, and other smaller works. Quantity was considerable, but what makes Mozart so remarkable is the amazing perfection of almost every single work he wrote from five years old until his untimely death. Mozart became a master of counterpoint, fugue, and the other traditional compositional devices of the baroque period, as well as all the Classical forms. He was also considered to be one of the greatest melodists of all time. His operas, in Italian and German, range from hilarious little vignettes to tragic masterpieces. His **Requiem** completed by his student Süssmayr is one of the greatest choral religious works in the entire canon. Along with the much older Haydn and the much younger Beethoven, (and, later, Franz Schubert), Mozart is the composer who brought the Viennese Classical style to its zenith.

❧ XIII ❧
MOZART'S CHARACTER

"Versification is, indeed, indispensable for music, but rhyme, solely for rhyming's sake, most pernicious."

— WOLFGANG AMADEUS MOZART

One of the odd manifestations of Mozart's genius was that

while he was a child, his odd behavior was tolerated because he was a child prodigy. Once he became an adult, many of these oddities began to be looked upon as strange, and off-putting. In addition, his father, who had stage-managed his career up to this point, was increasingly seen as an annoyance to many potential employers. Surviving letters from Empress Maria Theresa and her children show that he was something of an impediment to Mozart's gaining permanent employment. He was totally unaware of this, of course.

🕮

It must have been heartening to Leopold to hear Haydn's assessment of Mozart, when he said, two years before his death,

"I tell you before God, and as an honest man, your son is the greatest composer known to me personally and by name: he has taste, and, over and above this, the greatest knowledge of composition."

No father could fail to be proud of this kind of statement coming from the most highly regarded living composer. It must have been frustrating then, to Leopold and to Wolfgang, that his talents were not universally acknowledged by the aristocracy, who were in a position to hire him.

🕮

Mozart was also a small man, barely over five feet tall, thin and delicate features, marked with the smallpox scars from his illness. He was always well-dressed though, with a soft and pleasant tenor voice. He had prominent eyes but was otherwise relatively undistinguished looking. Being a short man in those days was a sign of poverty, and so it may not have helped him when looking for employment. He was also very fond of billiards, and when he was not writing in his bed, he wrote at his billiard table. He had a number of pets, including birds, a dog, and a horse, and he had a somewhat surprising fondness for scatological humor, which is often displayed in his letters.

৩⋇৩

When he wrote music, contrary to popular belief, he made sketches, and many of these were preserved after he died, but destroyed by his wife, who wanted to maintain the image of Mozart as a direct conduit of God. Mozart was a faithful Catholic, although he was also very interested in having a good time. According to some sources, he had a habit of speaking backward, which was confusing to many of his contemporaries, but which is a fascinating skill to have.

❧ XIV ❧
FURTHER READING

- Abert, Hermann. *W. A. Mozart*. Cliff Eisen (ed.), Stewart Spencer (trans.). New Haven: Yale University Press, 2007
- Deutsch, Otto Erich. *Mozart: A Documentary Biography*. Peter Branscombe, Eric Blom, Jeremy Noble (trans.). Stanford: Stanford University Press, 1965
- Solomon, Maynard. *Mozart: A Life* (1st ed.). New York City: Harper Collins, 1995

YOUR FREE EBOOK!

As a way of saying thank you for reading our book, we're offering you a free copy of the below eBook.

Happy Reading!

Printed in Great Britain
by Amazon

83613260R00079